Swatting Gnats

Also by the Author

Lee Alloway

Swatting Gnats

`

Ancient Eagle Press

Falls Church, VA

2012

This edition of Swatting Gnats has been
printed in the United States of America by
Ancient Eagle Press.

Library of Congress Control Number: 2012915191

For Jan

Swatting Gnats

December Storm

Warmed by solstice embers,
I watch the snow fall silently on moon-lit earth.
Unnoticed by the grass and leaves
As it blankets them against frigid night,
The snow covers crags and mudded trails,
Swells barren branches, fills the uneven and soiled,
Softens brambles by the pond,
Amplifies the moonlight with ice-blue luminosity
And brings serenity to the night.

So like the snow is my love as it falls gentle upon you,
Unnoticed in the rush of your day,
Offering a cloak of warmth should you feel the cold;
It covers your imperfections, magnifies your presence,
Turns your voice into a song and your nearness into a caress,
And makes vivid the colors of my life.

And from the embers of my own long night,
I nurture the love that gives meaning and light,
And draws me to you like a night creature to the fire.

My Eyes Are Grey

My eyes are grey.
They haven't always been this color.
When I was born my eyes had no color at all.
That frightened my daddy,
Who took me from my momma's arms,
And carried me outdoors, beneath the angry sky,
Where the grey of the storms flowed into my eyes,
And glares back to this day.
And sometimes, when you think you see
A tear on my cheek, you are wrong;
It's just the rain coming from that same storm,
Squeezing out of my eyes,
Because boys don't cry.
That's what my daddy says.

I'm tall,
But not too tall, like my uncle is,
Because tall people are slow of thought, like my uncle is,
Because there is no air up high.
And that's why my brother is slow of thought,
Because he sleeps way up high in the loft,
And giggles in the dark like a girl,
And is afraid of spiders, like a girl.
So when there isn't much to eat,
Because the rains don't come,
Momma gives me only a little food,
So I don't grow too tall
And become slow of thought.
That's what my momma says.

I'll have a working-man's face,

And that's much better than being handsome,

Because you can't trust handsome people,

Cause they're slick and they smile,

And they take your money,

And girls don't like handsome men,

Which would be OK with me right now,

But when I'm older I'll like girls,

And they will like my working-man face,

And my stormy eyes

That sometimes rain on my cheeks,

And the fact I'm not too tall,

And not slow of thought, like my uncle is.

That's what my grandma says.

But sometimes, I think

I'll walk to the edge of the world,

And I'll look down into an endless sea,

Shimmering blue, so clear you can see forever,

And I'll gaze into the quivering light,

Luminous like glacial snowpack,

Warm like the purple sunset,

Twinkling like a field of lightening bugs,

And I'll feast on magic fishes,

And grow tall and strong,

And I'll stare so hard I'll pull that sea right into me,

And it will wash the storm clouds away,

And my eyes will shine blue forever.

That's what I say.

Sea Pappy

The world is inside-out, and somehow I missed the joke.
I'm an orange being squeezed from the inside,
A balloon being inflated by a painted clown,
Soon to be twisted into a Dachshund,
A pirate's sword,
A crown.

I force the air from my lungs, but uninvited
It claws its way back, digging through
The alveoli snoozing in the corner,
Poking in the cupboard,
The sock drawer,
The bed.

Out and In, Out and In, Out and In.

A jellied pate with flowing braids, telling a tale,
Seen but unheard, the unblinking eye
Missing nothing in the dark,
Watching the watcher,
The doubter,
Sleep.

Though sleep is an illusion, a technicality captured
For analysis, as if disciples of Freud could
Mine the language of the brain and
Parse out the Id,
The Superego
The Ego.

Out and In, Out and In, Out and In.

So night stumbles forward, slicing the hours into
Indigestible morsels that lay on the pillow,
And lie about the truth, that time
Will not be denied,
Nor delayed in
The end.

And yet, because we can, we do; the servos and diodes,
The Botox and Viagra, glucosamine and Motrin
Elixirs that define Woodstock in decline,
Comfort us while we sleep everted
In our inside-out
World.

Out and In, Out and In, Out and In.

Elegato

Warm in the sunshine, in regal repose,
Here on the blanket you have prepared,
On two square feet of sovereign territory,
I lie and watch the birds at the feeder.

They are a distraction, nothing more,
But deep inside there is a primal calling,
Echoes of the time when our fates
Were linked, so long ago.

When I was the hunter, and they but toys,
Observe. Orient. Decide. Attack!
Feathers flying, the contest over in an instant,
A game of sport, no longer survival.

For you have served me well through eight lifetimes,
Offered food and shelter, never asked too much,
Brought me gifts of rubber rats and feathers on a string,
And never refused your lap when I demanded it.

You provided amusement for my few waking hours:
The dog to harass, carpet to eat, sofa to sharpen my claws,
And you to stalk, attacking from the shadows
As you carried food to the table.

In return, I allowed you to love me on my terms,
And brought you gifts of mice and crickets,
Left to be discovered by your bare feet,
A morning surprise more bracing than coffee.

But the mice are too fast now,
And the birds have nothing to fear
As I move slowly on wooden legs,
And pounce only in my dreams.

I travel by custom and reflex,
The light is dim and the food is tasteless,
Only the warmth of the sunshine remains,
And you, scratching my ears.

I do not sense the passage of time,
Beyond the cycle of wake and sleep;
I don't want to leave you, but I'm tired now,
And want to close my eyes.

So when you're ready, I am, too.
Help take away my age and my pain,
One last time, hold me in your lap and scratch my ears,
As you remind me of nine good lifetimes together.

Swatting Gnats

Dang! Take that!

Dang! Take that!

Dang nuisance. Pests. Swarming around my head,
Distracting. Annoying. They won't go away,
And won't come together.

> *"Peeling back the artichoke, savoring the meat..."*
> **"Reflecting in the pond, your face becomes my own..."**
> "Blowtorch rolling down I-10, grasshoppers
> frying in the pan..."

> *"You are my soul, torn from my heart one cruel summer night..."*

> "There once was a three-legged frog, in a hole in a hickory log..."

> "Morning sun dancing on dew-drenched fronds..."

Shut out the noise.
There is no music in my soul today;
The chorus taunts me.

"So gather in the dark of night and circle round my bed…"

"If Miss Pickel lived in Galena,
And Ana Tase dined on rutile, would Brookite be there,
And would anyone care
That Ty Tanium led for a while…"

"My mouth full of ashes, my heart washed with tears…"

"Our hands pressed against the glass, never touching…"

"Staring at the sun, I never saw you passing, yet heard the echo of your loneliness…"

"The saddest words are those I never spoke…"

"The nearness of you kindles joy and new light; my soul ascends…"

"How can this be, that time has no meaning…"

"The eyes look, and I see the world;
The mind considers, and I understand the truth;
Still the heart yearns, and my dream beckons."

Dang nuisance, like teenage kids:
Unruly, unformed, don't say what they mean,
With years of missteps before they mature.

To My Valentines, Past and Future

Time has flown, or yet flies to meet us
As our lives move together, move apart,
Exist in parallel, converge, merge,
Expand, contract and divert through life's mysteries.

We have been friends, family, strangers, lovers,
Have shared moments, hours, years or just a glance,
We have met, are yet to meet, perhaps will meet again.
Some of you have held my hand; all have held my heart.

I have written songs to you,
Celebrated you in poetry (locked closely away),
Talked to you in the quiet of the trees, the pounding of the surf,
Or only in the silence of my shell.

Each of you is part of the mosaic of my heart.
When it was torn, you were the balm,
When it sang with joy, you were the harmony,
And still we move together with every beat.

As past, present and future are entwined,
So are our lives. I am me because of you,
I love you as I know myself,
And will be of you when time comes round again.

I thought that I could scratch some line,

To woo and win my Valentine,

But each time I rewrote a verse,

The syntax got a little worse,

So I'll quit now and you will see,

I love you more than poetry.

The Acorn's Tale

Father brought me from St Louis in his pocket
where I was found, when Grandmother did
the wash, along with a penny whistle
and a paper ticket and string from
Father's lunch box.

They took me with ceremony to
the top of the rise where they buried me in
the earth, anointing me with water from
the well in propitiation of my sins, original and
yet to be.

We grew tall together, Father and I, both
nurtured by the prairie sun, steeled by
wind unrelenting and unimpeded from lands
far north, fed by loam from rivers reveling in the
thaw.

When Son appeared, Father would bring
him to me and they would play while
I kept the sun away. In time, Father built
a shelter in my limbs, where Son would climb
and watch.

A swing Father hung from my strong
arms, where Son and They and Others would
sit for long hours while they talked, shucked
peas, husked corn or sipped harsh liquor in
the moonlight.

And then there was She, who sat in the
swing with Son as they studied their grammar
and history and math, and learned over the seasons
the many lessons of life while I
kept watch.

In the sunlight, her hair was the mark
of Winter rye and her eyes, the echo of
August mornings, clear and blue. She moved
with grace and painted my world with oxalis
and Joe Pye Weed.

For twenty seasons they shared my knoll
on Spring afternoons and Summer mornings
when their talk and their laughter melted into
the sweet breath of zephyrs through my
boughs.

Until the day Son brought her to me,
and his tears washed my feet
and she stayed,
and stays, still
and Son comes no more.

The farm is fallow now.
The swing has fallen on one side,
and moves only at the bidding of the Kansas wind.
The shelter where once they played,
is fallen.

And I will wait the remainder of
my days in the silent field,
on the forgotten knoll,
and watch over
her.

With my Father, Dying

The world keeps thrumming, thrumming, thrumming
As it wobbles like a home-made dirndl
Spinning, if not eternally, at least through my eternity;

Like a transformer, thrumming, thrumming, thrumming
As it chews giant bites from the grid
And chums the power line with digestible pieces;

Like water over a weir, thrumming, thrumming, thrumming
With springtime rains leaving the pond,
Accelerating, growing, tumbling along its way;

Like the river, thrumming, thrumming, thrumming
Its belly swollen with snow pack, loess and dreams
Moving inexorably from mountain to valley to sea;

Like the wind, thrumming, thrumming, thrumming
Through mountain passes, racing across the plain
Moving forward, moving forever;

Like the respirator, thrumming, thrumming, thrumming
Pumping life into my father's lungs
Until the moment that I age, not by a moment, but by a generation.

North Star Setting
19 January 2012

Polaris set in the West tonight, and the skies wept.
For a lifetime and more he lived steady, unblinking,
Fixed in the firmament among a billion moving stars,
A guidepost for weary travelers on dark and bitter nights.

Never ostentatious, he paled next to the Big Dipper,
Who danced across the heavens, vibrant and alive,
Touching the horizons while he remained in his place,
And yet in all her travels, she was always fixed on him.

Orion was his alter ego, the warrior armed for battle,
Large in the night sky, complex and nuanced,
Locked in eternal combat with an insatiable foe,
Known by his girdle and scabbard.

In his later years, the Pleiades was his joy,
Shining brightly to his aging light,
Traveling with Taurus through the skies,
The seven beautiful together, beautiful apart.

For me, he was the only constant in an inconstant world.
When cold winds buffeted and currents pulled,
It was his light that marked my course.

When Sirens beckoned across hidden shoals,
And sang their seduction,
His music played more sweetly.

When gold and treasure opened themselves to me
For only the price of my soul,
It was his simple presence that saved me.

But tonight there is blackness where his light used to shine,
And silence where his song once echoed,
The stillness of the night seems less profound,
And the guiding star is no more.

Yet in the persistence of memory I see him still,
His place is set in the sky that I travel,
My way is lighted by his essence passing ahead,
My canvas painted by his brush.

Going Home

Walking the path where lately you walked
In the most mundane part of your day,
I see the formal mosaic of the floor,
The less formal mosaic of the cracked concrete,
The doors, locked and open,
The trees planted not by nature
And wonder what you see when you walk this path.
Or do you see nothing at all?
Is this an invisible universe to you,
So much a part of your day that it does not exist?
And am I also part of the invisible universe,
Acknowledged but unseen, a bit player in a supporting cast,
Another interchangeable, faceless person.

Shall I tell you what I see in these halls and these byways?
To me they are alive with the living and the dead,
They echo the history and the struggle,
And they glow with life because of you,
Because you have passed this way
And you have shared of yourself
And have become part of that history
And of the struggle,
And of me,
In the most mundane part of your day.

Layers

Leaving the office

    I spin the lock, shedding for the evening the

    Title, the Business Card, the Mask.

Changing in the gym,

    I leave the suit and tie in the locker,

    Dropping tension on the floor with the wet towels,

Three miles down the trail,

    Worries of the day have fallen aside,

    Kicked off the bike by the pumping of my legs,

At six miles,

    Hills strip away the ego, as younger cyclists climb

    With legs that my experience can't match,

Ten miles and nearing home,

    The weight of the office is off my shoulders,

    Melted away by sweat.

The steaming shower completes the job,

    Removing the lingering office armor,

    Sending worries into the watershed.

And then there is you,

    With a smile that disarms,

    And a hug that opens another door.

We read the menu, share some wine,

    And happen upon memories stacked neatly

    Like picture albums on a forgotten shelf.

Through dinner we select volumes,

    And gently probe the pages;

    I watch your eyes as retelling becomes reliving.

Walking home, your arm on mine,

    The moon an umbrella,

    We are wrapped in a glow that keeps the world apart,

Till alone together,

    We remove from each other the final artifice and conceit,

    And lie touching the hidden places of the body and the heart

    That are the essence of our beings.

The Creed

I speak the words, and lock one more stitch
Into the fabric of society that flows unbroken from my feet
Across eons to history's horizons and beyond,
An endless tapestry formed of rite and recitation,
Colored by the songs of a million cultures,
Some long forgotten yet indelibly part of the mosaic.

A congregant, professing faith to god;
A soldier, pledging blood to king;
A citizen, reciting love for country;
Words spoken a thousand times from a thousand hearts,
Words in unison, spoken so often and so loudly,
They are no longer heard, even by the speaker,
The clanging of a hollow bell.
And yet they bring comfort and community,
A shared faith, shared values, shared experience,
The adhesive that binds our lives,
Guardian against anarchy and chaos.

This echoes in the back of my mind
As I lie beside you, wrapping you in my arms,
Listening to your soft breathing, when I once again
Recite the creed that I have repeated so often before,
On so many lavender nights and so many quiet mornings,
A reflex almost autonomic, and yet so fundamental,
Always the same, yet always new,
Always a comfort, and always true,
As once again I say, "I love you."
I love you, too.

At Night

Laying in the dark, I listen to the house,
Itself a living organism that eats, breathes,
Produces heat, expels waste and, like a child,
Requires constant care and feeding.

I listen to my thoughts,
Which can be muted by the light
But will not be silenced, as they travel roads
Once taken and roads that stretch into the mists.

I listen to the sounds of you beside me,
Soft breathing, murmurs unformed,
The gurgle of your snoring, the rustle of the sheets,
And am at peace, for these are the sounds of love.

A State of Bearable Loneliness

Life at its core is a state of bearable loneliness,
An unspoken longing for that companion or that passion
That will bring meaning and fulfillment
As we toil beneath a colorless sky.

Ahhh, but when fate brings more for an hour, a day,
A decade or even for only a moment when two paths merge,
And we become so much more that we were,
That is the joy of life, and the food that sustains my soul.

You are, to me, that moment that fate has brought,
Unexpected, undeserved, and yet treasured
For the days and nights that are filled with you,
While the fog of bearable loneliness is lifted.

Sunshine pours into my heart, and music flows through my fingers,
The words will not be contained, nor the songs silenced.
The vaults have been opened, the curtains parted;
This I savor, warmth against frozen past and uncertain future.

I look into your eyes and see my own.
You were a part of me before we met;
With you my heart is whole and my spirit soars,
Barrel-rolling around clouds in the sky.

Yet I look in the mirror and see the truth,
That time is out of sequence and I am out of time,
The years have been kind but many,
As I have watched the world grow old.

So this must pass as a joy I cannot share,
But I will hold it always in my heart,
And it will sustain me when the fog returns,
A memory that makes life's loneliness bearable.

Vacation

Newspaper on hold – √
Mail forwarded – √
Yard to be mowed every ten days – √
Greenhouse watered, birds fed M,W, F – √

Clothes packed, truck loaded, and yet
The most important decision is still to be made:
With whom shall I share my summer at the shore,
And who stays, gathering dust and tempting the silverfish?

There's not time for everybody,
Some must be left behind.
And so to start. We start with
Drury, who advises, and I consent.

And Catton, a most civil friend,
And Tuchman (long left on the shelf),
Lest the storms of August rage,
And Karnow, to remind me of lost innocence.

Allende for the infinite beauty of her prose,
Buck to see the earth in another light,
And Tan to reimagine family,
With all its webbing and resiliency.

Then there are the hidden pleasures
Of Spillane and Turow and Carr,
And the comforting discomfort of Hemingway,
Steinbeck and Fitzgerald.

And of course, no summer could pass
Without a weekend with Faulkner,
Reminding me that I do not own books,
These books own me.

Sunday Drive

"You're insane,"
She says.

You're going to get us killed,"
She says.

"I know these people, you don't."
That's true.

To which I reply,
"I'm just following doctor's orders."

To which I add,
"He said to keep it elevated. I'm keeping it elevated."

"Well, put something over it,"
She says.

"A towel. A hat. Something,"
She says.

To which I reply,
"We don't have a towel."

To which I add,
"We only have boxes."

"They have guns,"
She says.

"And not just in the gun racks."
She says.

To which I reply,
"Really? What kind of guns?"

To which I add,
"When we move out here, I'll have to get one."

And again,
"Would an Uzi do?"

"You're insane,"
She repeats.

"And you're going to get us killed,"
She repeats.

We are driving down the road, city folk
Going to our weekend place,
Venturing into the country.

Wife driving, me resting my arm on the door sill,
Bandaged hand in the air,
Middle finger full of stitches, dressed for the dance,
An unintended salutation to our new neighbors.

Considering this new information, I observe,
"I like this place."

To which I add,
"I think I'll be mayor someday."

"If you live that long, you'll have only two qualifications,"
She says. "You'll be old,
And grey."

Mulberries

River of goodness rolling down my chin,
Springtime mulberries picked from the tree,
Overflowing my lips,
Sweet, warm and sloppy,
Like eager high school kisses,
Explored in the back seat of a 47 Dodge,
Big as the living room sofa, parked at the drive-in;
An earlier age, and innocent,
Before the drive-in died, its flesh peeling away.
Yet its bones remain, forty years on,
Standing vigil over memories
And mute speaker-posts assembled,
Rank and file waiting silently for the silent sermon
From the empty pulpit, while the coffers fill
With tumbleweed and plastic bags.

The squirrel chatters from high in the tree,
Pulling me back to today as he warily steals mulberries,
His eyes never straying far from me.
The catbird, discovering this bounty,
Calls her fledglings for a lesson in forage;
Wren and nuthatch sample and move on,
Chickadees, ever curious, pay homage but do not linger;
Blue jay watches, eyeing my prize,
But today I am the alpha consumer.
The low-hanging fruit is mine and I gorge myself,
A harmless indulgence, and rare,
Like those sweet, sloppy high school kisses,
Shared at a forgotten drive-in,
On half-moon summer nights so long ago.

Off Tucker Point

Sunday morning, while the God-people are still abed,
Before the jet skis shred the silence, their wake gnawing the shore,
I lay by in a cove, tie up in the shade of an overhanging cherry tree,
And give the kayak its head.

And we drift:

My kayak drifting perceptibly in the current and the breeze
To the end of its tether;
My mind drifting as well, moved by thoughts of impossibilities
Past, present and future.

Slowly the cove gives up its secrets.

Arrowroot march down the bank and into the water;
Spider webs lay littered with leaf mold and cadavers;
A kingfisher laughs in passing,
As a great blue heron takes umbrage and takes flight.

The bank is pock-marked with sanctuaries of all sizes,
Lifelines for mammals, amphibians and insects,
Each a diner…and a dinner in due course,
An unending cycle, but unhurried in my cove.

The stillness wraps around me like a blanket,
I close my eyes and am transported;
I see your eyes, walk with you for a moment,
Without saying a word to break the morning still.

While in the cove the frogs call me back,
The dragon flies hover, the turtle basks,
The minnows breach at the coming of the perch,
And I grow young on the waters of the Potomac.

Easter Sunrise

May your morning be filled with coffee and sunshine,
Your day with laughter and love,
Your evening with symmetry and peace;

May the happiness you give flow back into your heart,
Your smile be reflected on every face you see,
Your touch be always returned;

And may you have the courage to try,
To go beyond where I have been,
And soar where I have never dared.

Schrödinger's Cat is Out of the Box
and May Have Fled the State

Midnight passed some time ago, or so it seems to me
From where I sit in the lab with the clock mocking me from the wall.
Examining the evidence like a forensic detective,
I find uncertainty at every turn. I suspect Heisenberg,
Though my observations might have contaminated the evidence.
My investigation and my thoughts become increasingly random.
On the window, scrawled in glycerin, "$S=k \log W$".
Boltzmann must have had a hand in this!
Opening The Book, I dive into spacetime, seeking answers.
Running from the scene, I glance over my shoulder
And see the crime undone, one step back by one step back,
Discrete layers of time peeling away.
I see me at the computer, at the moment of the cat's escape,
Committing e-mail to the Internet;
I see me reflecting and revising, forming random feelings
Into thoughts that bring order to my perceptions;
As I run faster, I see vignettes, exchanges, data points
Without individual meaning, forming a reality in aggregate.
So where was the crime?
I turn and run back toward the lab,
Moving forward in space and in time,
Peering into the Future, which coexists with Past and Now.
Perhaps the future holds the key.
Perhaps the consequences will determine
The gravity of the offense and reveal whether
The crime was in the observation, or in the interpretation,
Or in the telling.

Let's Paint it Freckle!

I came home late from school one day and saw my daddy pack.
He said he's just be gone a while but soon be coming back.
He said that I should help my mom and hug her every day,
He kissed me and he held me then I watched him march away.

My mommy saw me crying and I saw her crying, too.
I was scared for just a moment, then she said, "Here's what we'll do,
We'll go down to the hardware store and here's the honest deal:
We'll paint your room the color of the way you really feel!"

"If you're happy we'll paint yellow like the sun up in the sky,
Or if you're sad we'll paint it like the grey cloud passing by,
You choose the color that you feel from black to shiny chrome,
And we'll do this every month until your dad comes marching home."

So we drove down to the hardware store and looked at what they had,
Their reds and greens were happy, but I was feeling sad,
The browns were getting closer and greys were almost there,
Then I saw the perfect paint: it was the color of Dad's hair!

And then his eyes winked at me from the row of greyish-blue,
And I told my mom we needed some…a little bit would do,
"We'll paint it on the dresser knobs and every day I'll see,
That when I look at them I'll see my daddy look at me!"

So we painted and we painted and pretty soon I found,
That Dad was in my room with me, his color all around,
With his tee shirt on my pillow and his voice in my bear,
I heard him say "I love you," though he wasn't really there.

A month went by and Mother came into my room one day,
And asked if I was ready to repaint another way,
I thought for just a minute and I knew what we should do:
"Let's paint some lines of white around some letters all in blue!

"Cause that's the place where Daddy works, I've seen it when you type,
Where Daddy's living now is in the country he calls "Skype."
But let's not change the dresser knobs cause Daddy likes to see,
When I'm playing in my room or when you say "Good-night" to me."

So we made my room a Skype-scape, the computer moved in, too,
Each morning we would talk to Dad, although his day was through,
Then one day I saw behind him, much to my surprise,
The knobs on Daddy's dresser were the color of Mom's eyes!

Before that month was over, Spring baseball started in,
Our team was just the best there was, we knew we'd always win,
The blue and white was still OK, but as the days got warm,
I was ready for a pin-striped room to match my uniform.

We planted flowers round the house and pumpkins by the tree,
We really made it pretty, working hard, just Mom and me,
So when another month went by we bought a can of red,
And painted flowers on my wall and high above my bed.

Then I met a friend named Sam and in a little while,
We'd have our lunch together; that would always make me smile,
So when it came the time to paint, you know what paint I chose?
I said, "Let's paint it Freckle, that's the color of Sam's nose."

Then one day Momma told me we could paint once more around,
Cause Dad was coming home real soon, he'd be back safe and sound,
So I whooped and then I hollered and I said, "Here's what we'll do,
We'll paint the room in stars and stripes of red and white and blue!"

And just like Mom had said, my daddy came back home to stay,
And he loved the color of my room…red, white and blue that day,
But then he did the strangest thing, I didn't understand,
When he took a chip of bedroom paint and held it in his hand.

He studied all the colors that had marked our months apart,
Now layer upon layer of the feelings of my heart,
Then he made it safe in plastic and it's snapped inside a locket,
And he says I'm always with him cause he's got me in his pocket.